For my parents, Sundar & Naran – SGC

Sital Gorasia Chapman is passionate about bringing math to life for kids. She worked in finance before becoming a children's author.

Consultant Steph King works with elementary educators to improve math teaching and learning in the classroom. She has written many math books for children.

Penguin Random House

Author Sital Gorasia Chapman
Mathematics Consultant Steph King
Illustrator Susanna Rumiz

Project Editor Robin Moul
US Senior Editor Shannon Beatty
Editor Laura Gilbert
Senior Designers Rachael Parfitt, Elle Ward
Production Editor Becky Fallowfield
Production Controller Leanne Burke
Jacket Coordinator Magda Pszuk
Managing Editor Penny Smith
Deputy Art Director Mabel Chan
Publisher Francesca Young
Publishing Director Sarah Larter

First American Edition, 2024
Published in the United States by DK Publishing
1745 Broadway, 20th Floor, New York, NY 10019

Copyright © 2024 Dorling Kindersley Limited
DK, a Division of Penguin Random House LLC

24 25 26 27 28 10 9 8 7 6 5 4 3 2 1
001–332643–Apr/2024

A catalog record for this book is available from the Library of Congress.
ISBN 978-0-7440-9128-1

DK books are available at special discounts when purchased in bulk for sales promotions, premiums, fund-raising, or educational use. For details, contact: DK Publishing Special Markets, 1745 Broadway, 20th Floor, New York, NY 10019
SpecialSales@dk.com

Printed and bound in China

www.dk.com

MIX
Paper | Supporting responsible forestry
FSC™ C018179

This book was made with Forest Stewardship Council™ certified paper – one small step in DK's commitment to a sustainable future. **For more information go to www.dk.com/our-green-pledge**

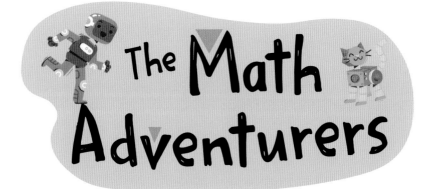

The Math Adventurers

Share a Camping Trip

One drizzly Monday morning,
the sky filled with heavy clouds,
Beep, and Boots the robot cat,
escaped the city crowds.

They traveled to a campsite
in a clearing in the trees.
They were greeted by a sunny sky,
and a warm and gentle breeze.

Camping

The forest was so lovely.
The air was fresh and clean.
They'd never been anywhere
so peaceful and serene.

They watched the bees and butterflies
dance among the flowers.
They marveled at the beauty
of nature's superpowers.

When we divide numbers or objects, we make equal groups. Can you see equal groups in this picture?

Beep and Boots watched the birds;
they listened to their song.
On a perfect day like this
they thought nothing could go wrong.

They wandered through the wilderness
and found an ideal place.
They pitched their tents side by side
in a sheltered, shady space.

Beep laid out the camping gear, divided it in 2.

The symbol for division is

"One tent for me," she said to Boots.
"And here is one for you."

10 tent poles and 20 pegs
to keep them safe and sound,
a rubber mallet to hammer them
into the solid ground.

Even numbers have the digits 0, 2, 4, 6, or 8 in the ones positions (the value of the digit that is farthest right in a whole number). They can be divided equally by 2 without any leftovers.

2 sleeping bags, 2 air beds, 2 pillows, and a blanket. Tableware and a feast to share for a special outdoor banquet.

Beep and Boots worked as a team,
starting with tent one.
They used up half the poles and pegs
until the job was done.

"Next, let's have a snack," said Beep.
"We really need a break."
They took the picnic basket
and sat down by the lake.

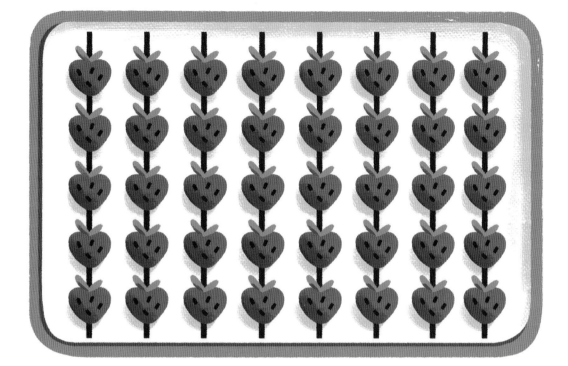

Beep laid out the strawberries
across a big white plate.
Some for now and some for later,
she divided them in 8.

When 40 strawberries are
shared equally between
8 kebobs, there are
5 strawberries on each kebob.

You can use an array to help
you solve division problems.
An array arranges objects in
equal rows and columns.
40 ÷ 8 = 5 and
40 ÷ 5 = 8.

When they were fully rested
and their tummies fully fed,
they started on the second tent.
"That's strange." Beep scratched her head.

The pegs had all gone missing.
Wherever could they be?
Beep looked under the bushes,
Boots in the tallest tree.

Some campers helped them search
around the campsite and the pond.
They divided into teams, and searched
the forest and beyond.

6 divided equally between 3 groups gives 2 in each group. Where can you see this division on these pages?

They couldn't find them anywhere.
Whatever would they do?
"I know!" said Beep. "We'll share the pegs."
She divided 10 in 2.

Dividing a number or a group of objects into 2 equal groups is the same as halving. What is half of 10?

The tents were not as stable
and Beep watched in dismay,
as a strong and sudden gust of wind
blew Boots' tent away!

Their friendly fellow campers
quickly rallied around.
Before Beep's tent was lost as well,
they pegged it to the ground.

Their forest shelter, safe at last,
was big enough for two.
What a busy day they'd had—
just one thing left to do.

They gathered around together
in the fading evening light.
Singing, laughing, sharing tales,
till it was time to say goodnight.

When 6 fruit kebobs are
shared equally between
6 campers, they each get
1 kebob. How would you divide
6 kebobs equally between
2 people? How would you
divide them equally
between 3 people?

If 6 fruit kebobs are shared equally between 5 people, there is 1 kebob left over. The leftover is called a remainder.

GLOSSARY

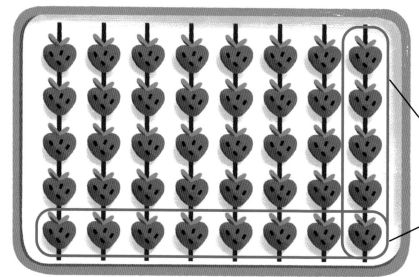

Array—a group of objects arranged in rows and columns

Column—objects arranged in a vertical line

Row—objects arranged in a horizontal line

Group—a number of objects

Division—sharing an amount into equal groups

Odd number—a number that cannot be divided equally into two

Even number—a number that can be divided equally into two

Divide—separate into equal groups

Equal—the same amount

Share—split into equal groups

Remainder—something left over when you can't divide equally

QUESTIONS

1. What is 6 divided by 2?

2. 10 ÷ 5 = ?

3. If 4 friends are sharing a box of 12 strawberries, how many strawberries will they each get?

4. If you have 10 socks, how many pairs can you make?

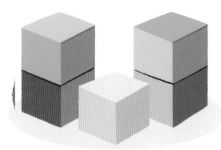

5. If you have 20 blocks and you want to make 4 equally tall towers, how many blocks do you need for each tower?

6. What is 50 divided by 5?

7. 50 ÷ 10 = ?

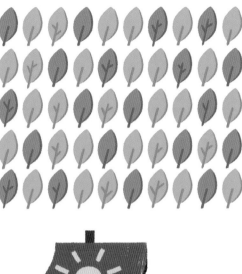

8. If a boat can carry 3 people, how many boats would you need to take 9 people across a river?

9. If you buy a bunch of 7 bananas and eat an equal number each day for a week, how many bananas do you eat on Monday?

10. Can you share 11 pencils equally between 2 people?

ANSWERS

1. 3
2. 2
3. 3 strawberries
4. 5 pairs of socks
5. 5 blocks
6. 10

7. 5
8. 3 boats
9. 1 banana
10. No. Each person gets 5 pencils, and there is 1 remainder.